your record.

'UE

he Excavation of the *Machault*

18th-Century French Frigate

alter
charchuk
d
ter
A.
addell

Parks   Parcs
Canada   Canada

Cover: Conjectural drawing of the *Machault* under sail. (Drawing by W. Zacharchuk)

The Excavation of the *Machault* :
An 18th-Century French Frigate

Walter Zacharchuk
and
Peter J.A. Waddell

**Studies in Archaeology
Architecture and History**

**National Historic Parks and Sites Branch
Parks Canada
Environment Canada
1984**

1079631

Price Canada: $4.75
Price other countries: $5.70
Price subject to change without notice.

Catalogue No.: R61-2/9-14E
ISBN: 0-660-11555-7
ISSN: 0821-1027

*E
199
.Z33
1984*

Published under the authority
of the Minister of the Environment,
Ottawa, 1984.

Editing and design: Jean Brathwaite.

The opinions expressed in this report are those of the author and n
necessarily those of Environment Canada.

Parks Canada publishes the results of its research in archaeolog
architecture and history. A list of publications is available fro
Research Publications, Parks Canada, 1600 Liverpool Court, Ottaw
Ontario, K1A 1G2.

Contents

Abstract

Between 1969 and 1972 the Underwater Research Unit (now the Marine Excavation Section) of Parks Canada's Archaeological Research Division investigated the wreck of the French frigate *Machault*, sunk in the Restigouche River, off Chaleur Bay in the Gulf of St. Lawrence, in July 1760 during the Seven Years' War. This was Parks Canada's largest and most complex underwater site and, at the time, the largest submerged-site archaeological excavation in the world.

The underwater work was as much a study of techniques and equipment as it was a study of the site itself, and Part Two of this paper describes the pragmatic approach taken to a major underwater archaeological task.

Four seasons of excavation of the *Machault* retrieved an enormous amount of material from the hold of the ship, as well as portions of the ship's structure and rigging, tools and munitions for operating and protecting the ship, and items reflecting human activity on board ship. The *Machault* has a very tight date of occupation and much of the cargo would not have been preserved but for the marine environment in which it sank. Although research on the recovered material has established that the ship was not fully laden when it went down, the artifact assemblage is large and demonstrates the broad range of goods provided to French colonies in Canada at the time, indicating some aspects of French trade patterns and colonial life in time of war. Moreover, the *Machault* has proven invaluable as a dating tool in the recognition of 18th-century material from land sites in Canada.

Acknowledgements

Naturally, an undertaking of the magnitude of the *Machault* project, and involving so many interest areas, could not have been completed without the cooperation of many people. Particular thanks must be given to the assistant director of the excavation, Robert Grenier, for his supervision of the barge-modification program; to Lorne Murdock, now with the Conservation Division, National Historic Parks and Sites Branch, who was responsible for overseeing and directing operations in what became a complete on-site conservation and treatment laboratory for the artifacts; to Robert Massé, now with the National Parks Branch of Parks Canada, for his administrative controls and for initiating the safety program; and to the divers on the project, some of whom worked on the excavation all four seasons and whose contributions extended beyond simply carrying out their regular assignments.

B. Bennett	U. Karkosa
M. Bergeron	R. Koop
S. Bern	G. Lapierre
J.R. Brabant	S. McDonald
M. Bujold	T. Metallic
M. Chandler	B. Palynchuk
D. Chevalier	E. Payne
G. Cumming	R. Piercy
F. Doucet	G. Purdy
R. Ferguson	P. Reilly
S. Gilmore	J. Ringer
P. Hallé	M. Sook
B. Herman	

People of the area became good friends and neighbours; their belief in the project made the task easier. Above all, special gratitude is due the late Burns Gregoire for his unswerving devotion and hard work. Catherine Sullivan, of the Archaeological Research Division, is also to be thanked for her assistance in the preparation of this report. Finally, many thanks to the material culture researchers, historical researchers, conservators and administrators whose perseverance, hard work, innovative efforts and written words have given a permanence to yesterday's events.

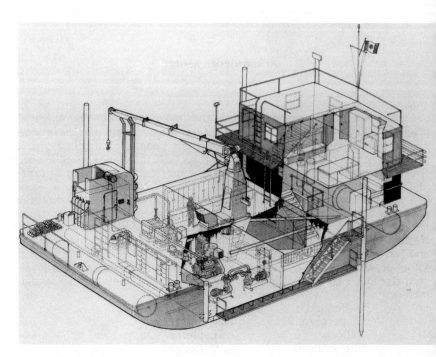

1   A steel dump scow, built in 1946, was modified for use as the excavation's main support craft. Below deck was located all of the machinery necessary for underwater excavation, such as two diesel electric generators and high- and low-pressure air compressors. The bow and stern served as storage areas for equipment, diesel-fuel tanks and compressed-air receivers. Above deck was a two-storey deckhouse in which were located office space, a galley and a head and showers. The pedestal crane, centrally located on the main deck and having an 85-foot-maximum reach, was one of the most important labour-saving devices used. The barge was held in place by four "spuds" that permitted vertical movement but arrested lateral motion during the ebb and flow of the tides.

Preface

Parks Canada became interested in underwater archaeology as an essential element of archaeological research in Canada during the 1960s. It was first used as a complement to land excavations at the Fortress of Louisbourg, Nova Scotia, a fortified town site on the Atlantic coast. As part of a study of the assault and defence of Louisbourg, divers surveyed the harbour bottom for the wreckage produced by a naval attack on the fortress. In 1966-67 a full-scale underwater excavation was undertaken on a gunboat sunk during the War of 1812 in Lake Ontario at Mallorytown. This was a fairly straightforward operation on a shallow-water site, under ideal water and climatic conditions, and demonstrated the many advantages of underwater sites. In comparison with most land sites, which may have many components, ships pose few chronological problems. Documentation can often be found because close records were kept of ships' passages, cargoes and structural modifications, and positive identification of a vessel can often be made. In many cases the contents of a sinking ship were not salvaged and through excavation it is possible to develop a more complete picture of human activity than on a land site. Organic materials are usually well-preserved on a wet site because oxygen is minimized in the environment.

At one time, Parks Canada had hoped to locate a series of different types of wrecked ships with known deposition dates over a broad range of time. Material recovered from these wrecks was to be used to create a data bank of information on material culture and ships' architecture. Creation of this data base would have entailed research on the full range of vessels from ocean-going merchant ships to boats used on inland rivers and lakes. This resource would have provided a chronological control for the material culture from land sites being excavated by Parks Canada. A further purpose of the undertaking was to create a record of assembly and structural details of boats because these particulars are not obtainable from archival records and drawings or from shipwrights' surviving models.

Unfortunately, underwater archaeological investigations are costly ventures. Personnel who can combine the technical skills of diver and archaeologist, and extensive surface support are absolute necessities for underwater archaeology in Canada, where the archaeologist contends with a short season and hostile environment. Tools designed to make efficient use of time and manpower are indispensible for archaeology under these conditions. In preparation for excavation of the *Machault* and with the intention that it would be the first of many underwater sites that Parks Canada would investigate, a steel dump scow was purchased from the federal Department of Public Works for use as a surface support craft. It required the addition of an elaborate assortment of power machinery and alterations to provide the necessary built-in flexibility to meet the varied conditions that might be encountered on the *Machault* and subsequent underwater sites (Fig. 1). Success in its design and modification is evidenced by continued use of the barge, with refinements, more than a decade later.

Archaeological excavation in all its forms is a destructive process. Underwater archaeology is particularly so because the hull of the ship is often damaged if the interior is to be excavated. Therefore, recording procedures proper to archaeological methods and theory are extemely important. In the case of the *Machault*, tides and currents stirring up the soft, silty, river bottom in the estuary lowered visibility underwater to the point of almost complete darkness. Consequently, provenience could not always be controlled, and photography and other recording methods requiring sight could rarely be used in the excavation.

As underwater work progresses during an excavation, structural parts and artifacts are removed from a stable and protective environment and exposed to a destructive atmosphere. Conservation of organic materials is expensive, time-consuming and largely in the experimental stages. Even under the best circumstances and with good facilities, it is difficult to plan for such problems as shrinking and twisting timbers, the loss of provenience information and the length of time objects are inaccessible when the conservation process involves long-term soaking in vats of chemicals. Conservation requirements took precedence over the material culture researchers' need to handle the *Machault* artifacts for research purposes, delaying the final reports on the artifacts.

From the *Machault* excavation it is clear that chronological type collections of material culture and vaguely defined questions on trade materials and social life do not justify the expense of an underwater investigation of its magnitude. However, the project was not without positive aspects. For example, the artifacts from the *Machault* contributed significantly to the body of knowledge now possessed by Parks Canada's material culture analysts, and subsequent underwater excavations by Parks Canada have benefited from experience gained from the investigation of the ship.

Underwater historic sites, a limited resource, are being endangered by non-archaeological interests, such as salvagers and sports divers. Although the *Machault* had not been disturbed, primarily because of the log-laden sediment in which it lay and the unattractive diving conditions, numerous other sites have not been so protected. The "adventure" that has come to be associated with sunken ships makes underwater exploration of wrecks an appealing hobby for recreational divers. Many are well-intentioned, turning their finds over to museums and other public institutions. However, they are, in effect, looting a site, with no obligation to a project or to the national heritage of Canada. As the diving community becomes better able to research and locate ships lost along our seaboards and inland waterways, and improvements in underwater equipment permit access to once inaccessible waters, the rate of destruction of underwater sites increases. The potential for the meaningful study of a site that has been looted to any extent is almost minimal. Further, artifacts that have lost their context are of little research value and are often in danger of destruction through lack of conservation treatment. Legislation cannot provide safeguards against underwater pothunting for enforcement of such laws would be extremely difficult with the amount of coastline in and around this country. At present the only protection afforded underwater sites is secrecy, which denies information to everyone.

The diving community has begun to set itself standards and objectives, and federal and provincial governments are becoming involved in various projects. But although these trends are encouraging, they must be strengthened and increased by everyone concerned or most of our underwater historic resources will continue to be treated frivolously.

Walter Zacharchuk
1982

Part One
An Introduction to the Project

Walter Zacharchuk

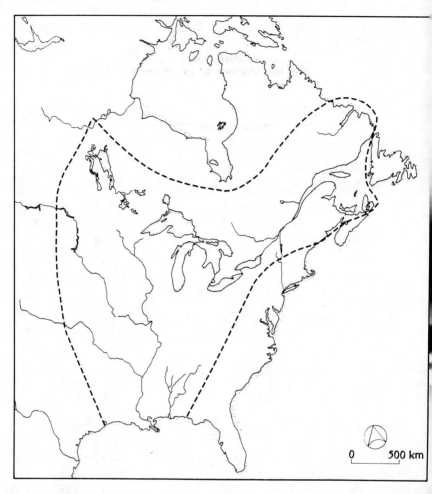

2 North America. The area within dotted lines was under French control by 1756; territories outside this corridor were in the hands of the British and the Spanish. (After Marcel Trudel, *Initiation à la Nouvelle-France* [Montreal: Holt, Rinehart, Winston, 1968], p. 79.)

Historical Background

In July 1760 the last naval encounter in the struggle for supremacy in North America was fought between France and Britain. The results of the British victory in this battle were that the supplies, munitions and men carried by the French fleet could not be used for retaking Quebec and eventually Montreal was forced to capitulate to the British. The story of this engagement, the Battle of the Restigouche, and the events that preceded it have been documented in various published sources. The following general summary relies on Lanctôt (1965), Lower (1949) and Morton (1963); information specific to the battle is based on interpretations by Beattie and Pothier (1977) and Litalien (1972).

The Treaty of Aix-la-Chapelle (1748) which ended the War of the Austrian Succession, gave Europe an uncertain peace but a time to consolidate; however, it did not put a stop to the hostilities between British and French colonies in North America. There, sources of friction were in part simply a continuation of the centuries-old animosity that existed between France and Britain, but were also the result of the fear and jealousy engendered by different languages and religions in proximity, competition for furs, fish and Indian loyalty, and an expanding British population threatening to upset French control of the interior — Lanctôt (1965: 143) sets the British population in North America at one million and the French at seventy thousand in 1756.

During the 1750s, while the mother countries were at peace, the colonies vied for supremacy on the Acadian frontier and in the Ohio Valley. In 1753-54 the French confirmed their hold on the Ohio Valley, which they needed to maintain communication beween the provinces of Canada and Louisiana (Fig. 2). But the expulsion of the Acadians in 1755 removed a population of potential French allies, and the loss of Fort Beauséjour to the British the same year cut off the overland route to Ile Royale (Cape Breton). France's access to its northern colonies was limited to the Gulf of St. Lawrence.

In Europe, war was officially declared by Britain on 7 May 1756 and by France a month later. To the British, a war that would give them an absolute monopoly on trade in North America was very popular. For France, on the other hand, fighting on too many fronts with inadequate funds, men and ships, the colony of Canada was a huge expense and, unlike the West Indies, one that did not return many revenues.

In North America itself, geography and the difference in population sizes dictated that to win this war, the French must hold what they had at the centre — that is, on the St. Lawrence — and hope that a French victory in Europe would preserve their interests in North America. However, Britain could afford to use its naval superiority on two Atlantic fronts and concentrate its efforts in North America on frustrating French attempts to provision its colonies by closing the Gulf of

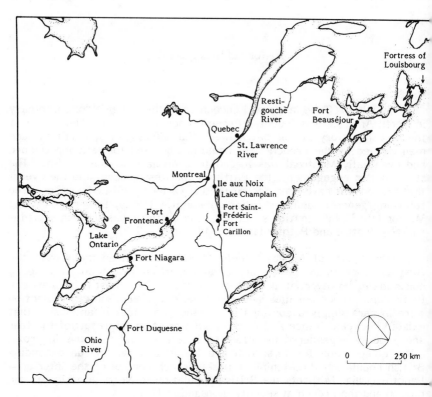

3 The main areas of Anglo-French conflict during the summer of 175!
are shown on this map, as is the site of the wreck of the *Machault* in
1760.

St. Lawrence. Accordingly, in 1758 a naval expedition was launched
against the Fortress of Louisbourg, capital of Ile Royale, which led to
the surrender of that town and of Ile Royale, together with Ile Saint-
Jean (Prince Edward Island). The same year, British colonial forces took
Fort Frontenac (Kingston) on Lake Ontario and Fort Duquesne (Pittsburg,
in the Ohio Valley. By December 1758, in spite of having held at Fort
Carillon and Fort Saint-Frédéric, Canada was isolated from Louisiana
and would have to defend itself at Niagara, Fort Saint-Frédéric, Montreal and Quebec (Fig. 3).

In the spring and summer of 1759 the British plan was to converge
on Quebec via the St. Lawrence, and on Montreal from the south and
west through Lake Champlain and Lake Ontario. The French response to
the Canadian cause was minimal; France could barely meet its own needs
in Europe and the British blockade was a considerable deterrent to
sending what could be spared by sea. All the relief that France would
send that season arrived in early May. In June the small garrison at
Niagara was overwhelmed by British and Americans, but French troops

retreating from Fort Carillon and Fort Saint-Frédéric met at Ile aux Noix and held, protecting the southern flank. In Quebec, Wolfe's attack was repulsed by Montcalm from mid-June until the British discovered a trail by which they could scale the heights to the Plains of Abraham. On 13 September 1759 Montcalm's small group broke before the larger force and fell back into Quebec. With Montcalm dead, his second-in-command a prisoner and the army in confusion, the governor of New France, the Marquis de Vandreuil-Cavagnac, withdrew to Montreal and ordered Quebec to surrender. On 18 September 1759 the British accepted the capitulation and stationed troops in the town.

In the provisional capital of Montreal the principal officers of New France and their troops gathered the militia and what munitions and supplies they could from the surrounding countryside for a spring attack on Quebec. In November, the British navy having returned home, Governor Vaudreuil sent a personal emissary, the Chevalier le Mercier, to Versailles to lay Canada's cause before the king and plead for the troops and supplies that would be needed for a siege on Quebec. Le Mercier sailed on the *Machault*, which had arrived in Canada in the spring of 1759. The *mémoire* that he carried detailed a plan for retaking Quebec and repulsing British reinforcements. Vaudreuil asked for at least 4000 men, plus cannons, mortars, trade goods, clothing for colonists and troops, flour, bacon and other foodstuffs, all to be sent under the protection of five or six vessels of war (see Beattie and Pothier 1977: 10-12). The preparations, he stated, had to be ready by the end of February and the attack on Quebec had to take place in May.

Concern over events in Europe, lack of money and realization of the urgency as well as the risks involved all contributed to a late and inadequate response by the home government. The ships were fitted out as cheaply as possible; crew members who had returned from the 1759 expedition refused to leave again until they received the wages due them from the previous journey; some of the calculations for stores were at fault and a delay occurred while these were unloaded. When the fleet finally left Bordeaux, the season was advanced and there were considerably fewer troops and less supplies than had been requested. The fleet consisted of six ships — the *Machault*, 500 (or 550) tons; the *Bienfaisant*, 500 tons; the *Marquis de Malauze* (or *Malause*), 354 tons; the *Fidélité*, 450 tons; the *Aurore*, 450 tons; and the *Soleil*, 350 tons — and several smaller ships that were being escorted. The *Machault* was, according to its size and number of guns, a fifth-rate ship; it was pierced for 26 guns, but may have carried as many as 32. (The number of guns varies from one account to another; Captain John Carter Allen reported 30.)

The second day out, an encounter with British vessels scattered the French and cost them two of their ships, the *Aurore* and *Soleil*. Heavy seas later took the *Fidélité*. In mid-May, in the Gulf of St. Lawrence, the remaining three members of the fleet captured a British ship bound for Quebec and learned that the British had preceded them up the river. Despite orders to abandon the mission to Canada and proceed to Louisiana and Santo Domingo in the event that the British had the advantage in the St. Lawrence, the French made for the Restigouche River in Chaleur Bay. Many of the troops in the fleet had served in Canada and the area was familiar to them. Equally important was the knowledge that the British had very little information about the channels in the bay. It would be a safe place to take on fresh water and bake bread in preparation for a long journey. Over several days the French encountered nine British vessels and succeeded in taking them as prizes. Once the French reached the Restigouche River, a messenger was dispatched on foot to the governor in Montreal, a camp was built, ovens were erected and food from one of the prize ships was unloaded. At Restigouche the French found a religious mission to the Micmac Indians active since the early 18th century, and an Acadian village of refugees which had formed around it. While the fleet awaited instructions from Montreal, the Acadians gathered to share the food and clothing that was being made available. These people created problems for the French whose main responsibility was the cargo sent by the crown. Supplies from France had not reached the colonies for some time and a hard winter had reduced many Acadians to eating beaver pelts. If supplied with arms and ammunition, the refugees could have afforded formidable resistance to a land attack by the British; however, a land attack was not expected and the refugees could instead have turned these arms against the French in the hope of getting more food and clothing by raiding the supply ships. The French tried to neutralize the danger from their allies by limiting the number of weapons they distributed. In addition, the French vessels were joined by an unknown number of Acadian privateers which had been interfering with British shipping in the area, and some fishing boats.

Instructions from Montreal did not arrive in time. The British had expected a French offensive and were prepared for it. When they learned of the presence in the area of armed French vessels, a fleet was dispatched from Quebec, and Governor Whitmore in Louisbourg sent the *Fame*, 74 guns, the *Dorsetshire*, 70 guns, the *Achilles*, 60 guns, and frigates *Repulse*, 32 guns, and *Scarborough*, 20 guns, under the command of Captain Byron, with orders to find and destroy the French ships. Contact between the French and the British occurred on June 22 and while the British lost a week searching for the navigable channel up the shallow river, the French prepared to defend their position. The supply ships were sent upriver to unload; some of the prize ships and Acadian boats were sunk across the channel at Battery Point, which was fortified and batteries were erected at other points as well. The concern of the French naval commander, Giraudais, captain of the *Machault*, was to secure his cargo. Although historic accounts are unclear on some aspects of the battle, it seems that Captain Giraudais adopted tactic designed to keep the British out of range of his own ships, since four of the five British warships were larger and more heavily armed than the largest of the French merchant ships. He might have hoped for nothing more than to save the king's supplies from the British by sacrificing his ships to block access up the Restigouche River. When the British pressed hard and an engagement appeared inevitable, Giraudais ordered the British prisoners from the prize ships, who had been interned in the hold of the *Machault*, to be transferred to the less vulnerable *Marquis de Malauze*. Every man who could be spared unloaded cargo from the storeships. The British engaged the French on July 5th. With the larger force and without the limitations on supplies and men that the French

18

had to contend with, a British victory was never in doubt. By 8 July Captain Giraudais was faced with the double problem of a dwindling supply of powder on the *Machault* and seven feet of water in its hold. The order was given to abandon ship. At about noon the *Machault* exploded and burned, and a few minutes later the *Bienfaisant* suffered the same fate, presumably at the hands of the French. After removing the prisoners, the British destroyed the *Marquis de Malauze* and set about to burn and demobilize all the French shipping that their guns could reach. This accomplished, they departed without, it would appear, further harassing the French and Acadian survivors who kept up a steady fire from the shore to discourage the British from landing.

Despite the loss of men, stores and transportation, the French managed to fit out some vessels and plunder British trade in the area and even to send at least two ships to France. When Montreal capitulated in September, Govenor Vaudreuil sent a small French force, accompanied by British troops on British ships, to Chaleur Bay to order the men there to lay down their arms. The French surrendered, and 196 soldiers and 80 sailors were loaded on ships to be repatriated to France. At the same time about 320 barrels of supplies and munitions found in the magazines at Restigouche were either destroyed or distributed among the inhabitants by the British, who also rescued some British prisoners, destroyed the cannons in the shore batteries, and tried to ascertain the number of Acadian and Micmac inhabitants in the area. In 1761 the British determined to clear the area of Acadians, who apparently had not ceased to interfere with British shipping to Halifax, Louisbourg and the St. Lawrence; however, some Acadians and Micmacs remained in the region and the Battle of the Restigouche continued to be a story of local interest.

Prelude to the Excavation

Nineteenth-century reports of residents who saw remains of two wrecks at extremely low tides probably refer to sightings of the *Marquis de Malauze* and the *Bienfaisant*. Some artifacts and timbers were said to have been salvaged from the vessels. In more recent times, the people of the area requested the Historic Sites and Monuments Board of Canada to assess the national historical significance of the Battle of the Restigouche with a view to commemorating the event. In 1924 a cairn was erected at Campbellton, New Brunswick, as a memorial to the last naval engagement between Great Britain and France for the possession of Canada. Between 1936 and 1939 the remains of what is believed to be the *Marquis de Malauze* were raised at the urging of Father Pacifique of the mission of Sainte-Anne-de-Restigouche. Federal government engineers found it impossible to salvage the entire wreck, but were able to bring up parts of the ship's cabin, masts, decks, hull and keel. The artifacts recovered during this operation included two light cannons, cannonballs, shot, and an oak barrel of pitch. The preserved remains of the *Marquis de Malauze* are on display at the Capuchin mission nearby and the vessel has been declared a historic monument by the province of Quebec.

Since the time of the battle, many artifacts relating to the supply convoy have been found ashore and in the shallows at the head of the bay. Newspapers and historical accounts describe and list several of these objects, and no doubt there are many more whose descriptions have not found their way into print.

In 1966 Parks Canada was persuaded that a survey and excavation of the wrecks might answer questions on the attribution and dating of artifacts being recovered from Canadian land sites with French occupation dates of roughly the same period: Fort Beauséjour, the Fortress of Louisbourg, and sites in Quebec City. As well, questions could perhaps be answered concerning maritime transportation and trade that could not be dealt with so directly in other ways. Although one ship, the *Marquis de Malauze*, was known to have been disturbed, it was expected that a great deal of 18th-century French material would still be contained on the other wrecks and that these artifacts could be used for comparative dating and to indicate the kinds of products that France was exporting to its North American colonies. In addition to the cargo remains, it was hoped that items that could be related to the crew would shed some light on a seaman's life in the mid-18th century. Efforts to find the remains of the fleet were begun.

Locating the hulls of the three French supply ships was facilitated by contemporary maps, there being three of the mouth of the Restigouche dating from 1760. Two of these, of British origin, have as their focus the marking of the navigable channel, although one contains the position of the ships during the battle (Fig. 4). The third map was

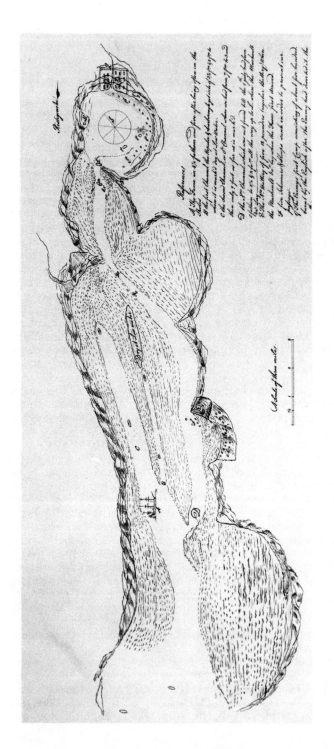

4 "A Draft of the upper part of Chaleur Bay, called Restigouchi, in the Gulph of S^t. Lawrence. by Captain John Carter Allen of His Majesty's Ship Repulse. Transmitted in his Letter of the 22^d July 1760.

References

A The Fame in 4–1/2 fathom and five after being often on the Sholes.

B The first Channel the Repulse & Scarborough got into of 3–1/2 f^m. & 2 f^m to where it is mark'd dry at Low Water.

C The Second Channel, or S^o. Channel where we had from 7 f^m to 3 and then only 9 foot as far as is mark'd.

D The N^o. Channel which was not found till the 5th july -- had from 5 fathom to 3-1/2 & 2 fa^m all the way up to L -- where the Machault &c^r Lay.

E The N^o. Battery of five 12 pounders (regular Battery) Where the Machault &c^r lay when the Fame first Arrived.

F five Schooners & Sloops sunk in order to prevent our passage.

G The Enemys first Camp consisting of about five hundred. burnt by the English after the Enemy had deserted it. the 4th int.

HH Sloops sunk in the narrows.

J The masque Battery of three nine pounders -- cover'd by a breast Work and many Small Arms.

K The upper N^o. Battery en Barbette. of 7. 12 and 9 pounders.

L The Machault of 30 Guns 13, 12 pounders of a Side.

M. N.&O. The Repulse, Scarborough, & Schooner (Arm'd).

P.P.P. The Bienfaisant, Marque Malorge Marquis de Malauze , and all the Small Craft which were destroy'd.

Q The Camp Consisting of 1000 Regulars, Canadians and Savages.

R Church and Priests House on S^o. point.

T The bay an Intire Flat boats ground"

(Public Archives Canada.)

23

executed by First Lieutenant Reboul of the *Machault*, and the area between Mission Point and Point à Bourdeau, where the ships were sunk, is very accurately drawn. Fortunately, the channel and the coastline have changed little in the years since the battle.

Using information contained in these maps and other documents to locate within very narrow limits the most likely areas of deposition, a preliminary underwater search was undertaken in 1967 for the remains of the wrecks. Divers found two hulls, one of which came to be identified as the *Bienfaisant*, and a collapsed stern section of another ship, tentatively identified as contemporary with the *Bienfaisant*. However, strong currents in the channel coupled with a lack of visibility and a bottom covered with the debris of 50 years of logging operations presented serious hazards to the safety of the divers as well as making a continued underwater search too expensive and time-consuming.

In an attempt to pinpoint the location of the third and largest vessel, as well as other elements of the fleet, a magnetometer survey of the channel covering the area of the wrecks was undertaken on the winter ice in March 1968. The hull that came to be identified as the *Bienfaisant* was used as a control point and the iron content of the wreck registered distinctly on the chart. Encouraged by the results of this experiment, a more extensive survey was planned for February and March of the following year. During those two months nearly two miles of the frozen channel were surveyed with magnetometers, one of which proved unsatisfactory because it was inconsistent and erratic in its operation. The final charting was done on an Elsec proton magnetometer, Type 592, imported from England. The instruments and their operators were carried on an old Bombardier snowmobile which towed it

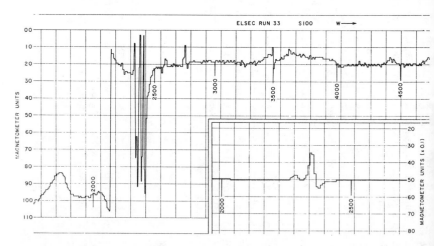

5   Facsimile of a portion of an Elsec magnetometer strip chart from the survey. The larger-scale inset is from the chart of a subsequent run on the same grid line. The anomaly of about 800 gamma at W2350 was caused by the remains of the *Machault*. (Compiled and drawn by A.E. Wilson.)

behind it the detector bottle mounted on a brass-fitted wooden toboggan. The estuary was surveyed with theodolite and a chain, and a grid was established over an area of the channel 1000 ft. wide and 10 000 ft. long. The grid was laid out on the ice with wooden pickets in 100-ft.-by-500-ft. rectangles, and magnetometer readings were taken at 25-ft. intervals running the length of the grid (Wilson 1970). A number of obvious anomalies were charted and 13 were selected for underwater investigation in May 1969. Of these 13, four were labelled because of their magnetic importance. 1M proved to be the *Bienfaisant*; 2M was tentatively identified as the *Machault* (Fig. 5); 3M was an anchor, which was raised; and 4M was determined to be a jettison site from the period of the battle, possibly the result of a ship's running aground or attempting to reduce its draught for further penetration up the Restigouche channel. Several other anomalies were briefly investigated before attention was concentrated on 2M, which seemed to be the largest and least disturbed of the wrecks. Historical maps and the process of elimination indicated that this should be the *Machault*, flagship of the convoy. The timbers that could be seen indicated that large portions of the ship were deeply buried in the deepest part of the channel, thus protecting what remained of the cargo and promising to yield valuable information on marine architecture in the mid-18th century. The site was selected for extensive excavation and four seasons of work were projected. The first three years were to concentrate on the excavation of artifacts from the wreck and the fourth on raising portions of the ship's structure.

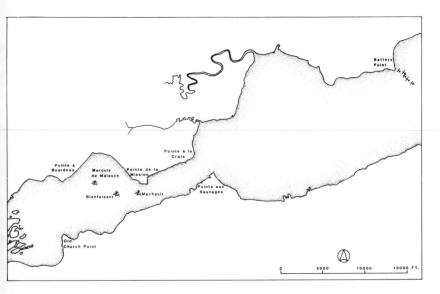

6   Detail of the Restigouche River encompassing the major finds.

Part Two
The Excavation

Peter J.A. Waddell

7 Looking south across Chaleur Bay toward Sugar Loaf Mountain above Campbellton, New Brunswick. The barge is anchored directly over the *Machault*.

Introduction

The first three years of work on the *Machault* were devoted primarily to excavating the ship, and the major objective of the final year was the recovery of significant architectural remains of the ship's hull for analysis and display.

As underwater archaeology is a relatively new discipline and since wreck sites vary greatly, no precise outline of procedures covering every situation was available to guide archaeologists investigating the *Machault*. Excavation problems required the implementation of specialized techniques and mechanical aids on a trial-and-error basis. Those which proved the most effective were continued and refined as work proceeded. In many instances existing tools had to be modified and in some cases new tools had to be developed to meet the demands of the site.

During the four years of excavation in the Restigouche over 5000 hours were logged underwater:

	Total Diving Time (Hours)	Total No. of Dives	Average No. of Hours per Dive
1969	813	416	1.95
1970	957	381	2.51
1971	2726	900	3.03
1972	712	303	2.35
1969-72	5207	2000	2.60

Approximately 90 per cent of the dives in 1972 were directly related to cutting and raising the timbers of the *Machault*.

A diver usually worked one underwater shift in the morning and a second one in the afternoon. The first half of a shift would normally last from one and a half to two hours; the twin air tanks used would sustain most divers that long, depending on tidal conditions, water temperature, degree of physical exertion and other such variables. After a brief rest and change of tanks, a diver continued work for up to two more hours until his shift was completed. This was the standard for most working dives although individual dives varied from as little as 15 minutes to in excess of seven hours.

Diving Conditions

Underwater working conditions at the mouth of the Restigouche River were the most difficult of any excavation undertaken by Parks Canada's Marine Excavation Section. Visibility was bad. A conservative estimate would put a minimum of 50 per cent of the diving time at zero visibility, total blackness. Being able to perceive an object of any size, shape or colour at three feet was considered good visibility; seeing anything beyond eight feet was a rare occurrence. Several factors were thought to have contributed to these conditions:

- Raw sewage and industrial waste were dumped into the Restigouche.
- Extensive sediment has been created by the logging operations conducted on the river for over 50 years.
- Rainfall causes Restigouche tributaries to overflow, resulting in an increase in the amount and movement of sediment. This was especially noticeable 12 to 48 hours after a heavy rainstorm.
- Wind, especially in the shallows, churns the water enough to significantly disturb bottom sediment.
- Currents are often strong enough to create extensive sediment movement.
- Strong tidal action, especially spring tides, also contributes to extensive sediment movement.

As often as not, the excavations were conducted strictly by touch.

The depth from surface to river bottom around the *Machault* ranged from a low of seven feet to a high of 25 feet, depending on wind and tide conditions. Excavations varied from several inches to over seven feet below the surface of the riverbed. Depths on the other Restigouche underwater sites never exceeded 25 feet, but were likely shallower than seven feet during spring tides. Water depths were never great enough to create a threat to divers from decompression sickness; however, there was always a possibility of direct pressure-related accidents.

Water temperature ranged from a low of 45°F in May and October to a high in the mid-sixties from mid-July through mid-August. The average water temperature for the diving season was approximately 50°F. Diving hours were thus temperature-limited during the early and closing stages of the operations. Mid-summer conditions were quite comfortable for underwater shifts extending three to four hours.

The contaminants in the Restigouche were responsible for more than minimal visibility underwater: the divers developed chronic external ear-canal and sinus infections which were most pronounced in 1969. A Department of Health and Welfare physician visited the site and indicated that the ear infections were external, but serious enough to keep over half of the crew from underwater work. This prompted an examination of bacterial levels in the waters by the medical authorities as well as a search for a method of preventative health care for the problem. In 1970 the ear and sinus infection problem again made itsel painfully evident and Health and Welfare personnel came up with pre-an post-dive general preventative measures that significantly decreased th rate of affliction to a point where mass occurrences of the infection were eliminated. The divers subjectively observed that the incidence o infection was substantially related to water temperature and length o exposure underwater. Specifically, the infections seemed most pro nounced during July and August when the water temperature an bacterial levels were at their height, and the dive times were extende due to warmer water.

Tineal infections, especially tineapedis, were not uncommo amongst crew members, again due primarily to the river pollutants a well as the constant wetting. General cleansing recommendations wer made by the Occupational Health Division and tineal infections wer kept under control thereafter.

These infections were the only significant medical problems t develop during the four years of the project.

Probably the greatest single danger to divers was the threat o injury or entrapment from mechanical sources due to the profusion o airlifts, pipes, hoses, grids, crane ropes, hydraulic lines, etc., as well a the wreck timbers themselves. Moreover, semi-buried logs served a catch-alls for other logs and debris, creating mounds and subsequentl hazards compounded by the zero or near-zero visibility. Water-soake logs, too light to rest on the riverbed but too sodden to reach th surface, would continually drift through the site, interfering with work and sometimes dislodging equipment installed on the bottom.

Despite the extremely difficult diving conditions, more than 500C diving hours were logged without a single mishap. A set of formal safety standards and regulations evolved over the life of the project, but the general consensus of the divers concerned was that, especially in the earlier years, the record was as much a result of good fortune as it was of prudence.

Dress

Divers used standard scuba gear. Twin 71.2-cubic-foot steel tanks coupled to a two-stage single-hose regulator formed the basic scuba system. The remaining standard paraphernalia consisted of wet suit, safety vest, knife, mask, fins and weight belt although variations and additions were investigated. In using this standard scuba gear, the divers normally worked untethered.

Dry suits were used sporadically during the 1969 season, but their combination with scuba equipment as opposed to hard-hat equipment was not successful. The neck-entry dry suits proved exceptionally unsatisfactory as the neck seals leaked and the suits' European design was ill-proportioned for most of the divers. Both factors resulted in considerable loss of body heat and this style of dress was abandoned for underwater operations although it did prove very effective for wading and other non-submersion work such as the erection of shallow-water sighting guides.

The most commonly used diving dress was the 3/8-inch wet suit. In some suits the zippers were removed and the seams glued, reducing water transfer within the suit and increasing insulation efficiency. The application of heavy elastic bands around the suits at the wrists and ankles was also helpful in reducing in-suit water circulation and concomitant cooling.

As one might expect, divers' hands and feet were most affected by colder water and heat loss was most critical in their hands. Gloves of 3/8-inch neoprene could not overcome the problem, further complicated by the fact that divers often had to remove their gloves to perform tasks requiring high degrees of manual dexterity. Chilling is more serious than simply causing discomfort for a diver who cannot manipulate his fingers could become a serious hazard to his own and other divers' safety.

With water temperatures above 50°F, as in July and parts of June and August, it was often possible to work for several hours without gloves at all. When protection was required from broken ceramics and other hazards, standard household dishwashing gloves and rubberized canvas gardening gloves were employed. The rubberized canvas offered the greatest protection against abrasion while the dishwashing type allowed greater sensitivity of touch in the persistently limited visibility of the Restigouche.

The summer of 1971 saw the introduction of European variable-volume one-piece dry suits (Fig. 8) to the project. The inflatable neoprene suit had watertight zippers and seals at the wrists and neck. The nylon-fleece underwear worn with the dry suit proved to be effective in reducing chilling, thereby increasing diving time and working efficiency. This condition persisted as long as the watertight seals could be maintained. Project divers soon learned that a truly "dry" suit is nonexistent.

8   Variable-volume diving suits were introduced to the Restigouche excavations in 1971. Communication equipment was introduced in 1972.

The three-finger mitts for the variable-volume dry suits, although decreasing the divers' manual dexterity, were more effective in preventing heat loss than common wet-suit gloves. Nevertheless, in water temperatures of 45°F and below, numbing of the divers' hands was still a problem and no effective solution was found.

An attempt was made during the final year of the project to adapt a wet suit to an open-circuit hot-water heating system. Hot water was fed to a diver's suit from a standard, residential-type water heater via an ordinary garden hose. The results of initial test dives were very promising, but unfortunately time did not permit further development.

Preparation for Excavation

Search Techniques

Search procedures varied according to the target's shape, size of the target area, degree of visibility underwater, and other factors. If the area was reasonably limited, i.e., less than 150 feet square, a circular search was often undertaken around an anchored buoy that marked anomalies noted during the 1969 winter magnetometer survey (see Wilson 1970: 89) on the ice-covered river. A diver engaged in this type of search was tethered by a rope to the buoy or, currents permitting, repeatedly surfaced to check his bearings in relation to the buoy and adjust his search accordingly.

If a larger area was to be searched, the most common method used was simply to ride the current. This was often employed in relocating the sites in the spring as permanent marker buoys could not be installed over sites in the shipping channel and buoys over other sites would have been damaged by the logging booms which passed frequently. A boat would carry the divers upstream from the target area, drop them off and then drift downstream to pick them up after their pass through the area. If unsuccessful, the divers would be dropped off upstream again to make other runs parallel to the previous one. The process was continued until the site was located. Several times the anomaly location procedure was accurate enough that a search was not required. This was the case with the *Machault* as the target buoy anchor landed between futtocks on the starboard side of the wreck.

Under ideal conditions only a few feet of the wreckage of the *Machault* was visible at any one time, but the initial impression of the site was one of an enormous amount of scattered wreckage. In order to obtain an idea of the ship's overall dimensions, a series of floats was tacked to the protruding ends of the starboard and port frames. From the surface position of the floats it could be determined that the main ship skeleton (keel-keelson-frames) was approximately 100 feet long and that it ran generally north-south. This information, the frame dimensions and the extent of the wreckage confirmed that this site was most likely that of the *Machault,* the largest of the three major French vessels involved in the Battle of the Restigouche. The initial dive also showed promise of artifacts as simply fanning the sediment in certain areas revealed cannonballs and wineglass stems.

Site Clearance

Some of the frames of the *Machault* protruded from the sediment as much as 3-1/2 feet; others were barely above river bottom. These protrusions were natural catch-alls for logs, pulpwood, trees, branches

and other debris so full-scale operations had to begin with the removal c
enough of this material to permit the placement of the excavation grid:
This required over 43 diving hours in 1969 and a comparable number c
hours was required for clearance in subsequent years, attesting to th
changing conditions of the river.

Logs were half-hitched, up to ten at a time, along lengths of rop
and then pulled to the surface by hand. Significant amounts of woode
debris were also removed from subsurface levels as excavation prc
ceeded. Often the use of hand and power saws was required to cut th
larger logs prior to their removal (see "Equipment"). After several corc
of wood had been accumulated in the support skiffs, it was take
approximately half a mile from the site and dropped in another channel.

In 1971 and 1972, debris removal was greatly simplified by the us
of the deck crane, when available. The amount of logs removed was the
limited only by the length and strength of the ropes employed.
addition it was not necessary to spend several hours dredging or airliftin
overburden from a log protruding into the site; only enough had to b
cleared to allow a rope to be attached to the log, which could then b
extracted mechanically.

Grid Installation

An investigation of the wreck site revealed that the keelson wa
quite prominently uncovered at its south or downstream end. A hole fc
an iron pin that was part of the keel-keelson assembly and approximatel
eight inches from the southern end of the keelson was a logical an
convenient main datum point from which to orient the grids. Providin
it was not broken beneath the silt, the keelson would serve as a constar
reference for systematic excavation of the ship.

Galvanized pipe, 3/4-in. in diameter, was used to make 10-ft.-by
10-ft. squares which were further subdivided into 5-ft.-by-5-ft. quarter
which formed the basic excavation unit or suboperation. The 10-ft.-by
10-ft. sections were constructed with 1-in. galvanized couplings welde
into each corner so that several grids could be mated at the corners b
passing a 3/4-in. pipe vertically through the couplings. The first grid wa
attached to the main datum point and successive grids were place
parallel to the first, north along the keelson, establishing a convenier
reference. Grid sections were then successively installed to a distanc
of 30 feet out from the keelson. In most areas these boundarie
encompassed the major portion of the wreckage; where they did no
successive extension units were installed until sterile riverbed wa
encountered.

The installation of the 10-ft.-by-10-ft. grid sections was tim
consuming but presented no great difficulties for two persons. A singl
diver could probably have accomplished the task in clear water althoug
positioning a section was often awkward because of the changing botto
contours, protruding ship structure, bending pipes and a multitude c
minor problems.

To keep the grid horizontal, sections were allowed to rest c
broken futtocks of appropriate heights. If none were available, the gr

corner-connecting rods were extended down to solid structure and the grids clamped at the appropriate height. The grids were attached to the reference keelson by metal spikes.

An alternate method of grid attachment was placing an inverted U frame over the keelson and clamping it to the keelson sides; however, this method was not developed in time for an extensive evaluation. Its use at the close of the 1971 season was satisfactory, but it was not adopted in 1972 since the use of grids was then limited to providing only a very general means of orientation to the divers clearing and cutting the hull.

In 1971 and 1972 a 1-1/2-inch galvanized reference pipe was installed along the keelson and extended 20 feet past the keelson extremities. Three-quarter-inch couplings were welded at ten-foot intervals along the pipe to accommodate the vertical corner-holding pipes of the grid. This pipe had a dual function: it kept the north-south grid reference in a constant place on the keelson, and it formed the attachment point for grids when work extended past the fore and aft limits of the keelson.

In 1971 the excavation switched to the use of 10-ft.-by-30-ft. grid sections (again divided into 5-ft.-by-5-ft. suboperations) constructed of 2-in.-square steel tubing for its perimeter and 3/4-in.-square steel tubing for its interior divisions. These units provided a much more constant and stable reference due to the decreased number of corner connections and greatly increased rigidity and strength. Considering the area covered and the overall advantages gained, the larger sections were more efficient for both installation and use. They were placed at right angles to the keelson where they were attached in the same manner as the 10-ft.-by-10-ft. sections. When the area enclosed by one unit was completely excavated, the grid was leapfrogged ahead to the next vacant position and this process was continued down the length of the ship.

Two or three divers were generally employed in the installation of the 10-ft.-by-30-ft. sections, which was greatly aided by the use of the deck crane. A diver would attach a rope sling to a grid at points equidistant from the centre of gravity, allowing the grid to be raised horizontally and manoeuvred into its new position. The work was immeasurably aided by the use of underwater communication units (see "Equipment") which enabled divers to communicate with each other and to guide the crane operator without surfacing.

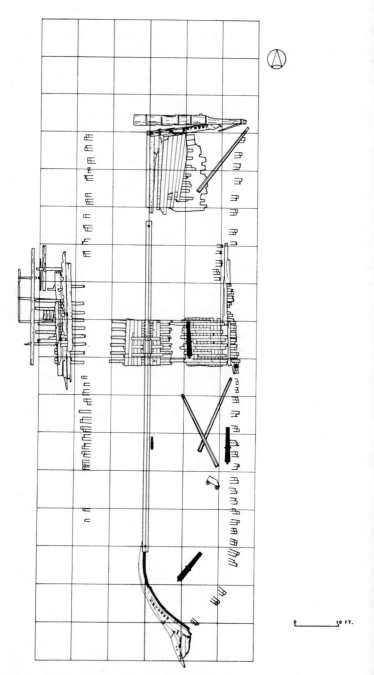

9 As-found illustration of the *Machault* based on underwater drawings and drawings of selected raised structural elements.

Underwater Recording

Following the excavation of a lot, the excavator attempted a scale drawing of the structural remains on 8-1/2-in.-by-11-in. Mylar draughting sheets on which a standardized scaled grid of a 5-ft.-by-5-ft. suboperation was printed. The most popular scales employed were coilable metal rulers although rigid scales and carpenters' folding rulers were often used, depending on circumstances. Because of extended periods of zero visibility, drawings were often based on tactile observations alone. The diver obtained a measurement on a scale and then rose (often to the surface) until visibility increased enough to permit reading and recording the dimension. Another technique employed was to record marks directly on a scale, but only a limited number of measurements could be taken at one time with this method. These procedures were repeated any number of times depending on the complexity of the structural remains.

Plan drawings were of greatest importance although, where practical, an elevation of the structure or other feature was obtained. Attempts were made to assemble composite drawings from individual lot drawings, but discrepancies in measurements were immediately obvious between adjacent lots, and some features which ran through several lots were often missing or displaced. Wreckage which had collapsed onto the hull was subject to movement once the supporting fill had been excavated and a degree of error in the zero- to low-visibility recording techniques was also to be expected. Nonetheless, the drawings were continued as the information was invaluable for specific details as well as general site intepretation.

Some composite drawings of major hull sections were done after the sections were raised. The drawings were useful in completing as-found illustrations of the entire hull (Fig. 9) and in showing some of the original spatial relationships of the raised sections.

Equipment

Jetting Hoses

Jetting hoses were used occasionally throughout the project. Small three-horsepower gasoline engines were used to drive deck-mounted general-purpose water pumps with capacities up to 800 gallons per hour. The major operational difficulty was the natural backward thrust created at the nozzle end of the hose. Since the diver had only slight negative buoyancy, it took only the back pressure from the discharged water to move him. Even if he could brace himself on the bottom, the nozzle itself was very difficult to control. In 1972 the problem was overcome with two brass balanced high-pressure nozzles which incorporated calibrated orifices that propelled small jets of water in the opposite direction to the main nozzle flow, thereby neutralizing the backward thrust of the main jet. The 2-1/2-inch rubber-lined canvas fire hoses generally used were satisfactory except when long lengths of hose were used close to the support craft, in which cases kinking became a serious problem.

The jetting hoses were generally used in previously tested, non-artifact-bearing areas to clear excessive overburden from buried sections of the wreck and to relocate previously excavated structural elements, such as the keelson, which had been covered by the winter's accumulation of silt.

The major drawback to the use of water jets was the fact that the agitated silt eliminated any visibility that was present, creating the risk of jetting into unexcavated areas. Visibility was also eliminated for other divers in the immediate vicinity or downstream from the operation. As an excavation aid, jetting was not generally effective for Restigouche conditions although in clearing previously excavated areas it was very efficient.

Suction Dredges

Suction dredges or "suckers" were used only during the 1969 excavation season. These units, which operate on a water-stream Venturi principle, were run by the same pumps that ran the jetting hoses. The 8-foot-long suction dredges were made of tapered aluminum tubing with a five-inch-diameter intake, seven-inch-diameter exit and a 45-degree elbow at the intake end. Water was forced via a flexible hose to a two-inch-diameter aluminum pipe mounted outside the larger pipe. The small pipe entered the larger one near the intake and directed the water towards the exit, creating suction.

A more powerful commercial fire pump was also used to operate two suction dredges simultaneously with a great reserve of power, but the larger pump could not be operated at full throttle as the backward thrust quickly put the units out of the divers' control. Using a gate valve on the input line so the divers could adjust the flow themselves was suggested as an alternative; however, it was not sufficiently investigated since the concept of dredge excavation proved to be unfeasible, again in part because of limited visibility. The chances of a diver inadvertently dredging up an artifact were considered too great, especially as the suckers expelled the discharge underwater and artifacts could be irretrievably lost.

An initial attempt was made to collect the overburden discharge in modified 45-gallon drums. The drum lid and bottom were cut out, one end was lined with half-inch wire mesh and the other end tied over the sucker exhaust. The theory was to allow the drum to fill, stop the dredge, raise the drum to the barge and screen the discharge for artifacts. Numerous factors, including the uneven riverbed that made the drums liable to spill, time lost in zero visibility and difficulty in raising the drums by hand, led to the abandonment of this system.

During periods of good visibility and adequate current to dispose of the discharge, the suckers were effective, especially at the jettison site (4M) where test trenches rather than formal excavation techniques were employed.

Airlifts

Airlifts were the main excavation tool employed at Restigouche. More diving time was spent operating these devices than on any other phase of the underwater work. An airlift is basically a long, hollow tube supplied with air through a manifold a few feet from its bottom end. Air entering the tube under low pressure (approximately 50 to 100 psi) rises through it toward the surface, creating a suction effect. This action combines with bubble expansion (due to decreased hydrostatic pressure on ascent) to create suction at the lower, or intake, end that is sufficient to excavate. Thirty-foot, four-inch-diameter PVC piping proved most satisfactory after a variety of experiments with three-inch to six-inch and eight-inch piping. Air was channelled from the compressor into the PVC tube through a one-inch-diameter galvanized steel pipe. A standard gate valve at the base of this pipe allowed a diver to start, adjust and stop the flow of air.

Prior to commencing work, each diver would attach 15 to 30 pounds of weights to the base of his airlift to stabilize the unit. Another method of securing it was to tie it onto a securely attached grid. A four-inch-diameter hose, six feet to eight feet long, was attached to the intake to enable the diver to reach all of his excavation area.

In the upper strata, with heavy overburden, the diver would use both hands to force the flexible intake hose into the mud and debris. Large rocks and twigs had to be cleared by hand. The abundance of twigs and rocks in the overburden caused the airlifts to clog, but fortunately most such blockages occurred within the hoses which the divers could easily detach and clear without surfacing. As artifact-bearing strata were approached, the diver would hand-feed the intake, which allowed him to discern the presence of artifacts as most of this work was done in complete darkness. Delicate artifacts and those the airlift would not accommodate were carried to the surface by hand, usually just after being located. The alternative of having a plastic laundry hamper, metal bucket or other container close by to store material was not always desirable since other divers or surging airlifts and currents could dislodge and spill the containers without anyone realizing it. Before surfacing, the diver would shut off his airlift to ensure that it would not dislodge strata or artifacts with its surging or take up material that would block it.

Perhaps the biggest drawback to airlifting was the lack of sufficient suction during mid-and low-tide periods when the airlifts worked at only a fraction of their high-tide capacity and had a much greater tendency to become obstructed due to the reduced hydrostatic pressure on the intake as well as the increased "dry" height to which the effluence had to rise. Efficiency at the lowest tides was so poor that airlifting was often stopped for up to two hours. This contrasted sharply with efficiency during the highest of the high tides, which enabled loads as dense as six-pound cannonballs to be carried to the surface screens via the airlift. Nonetheless, airlifts were overall the most effective excavation tools employed.

Suboperations were excavated as deep as seven feet below river bottom with the aid of airlifts. The physical problem of both a diver and the angled airlift within a five-foot-square lot was overcome by the flexible hose extension on the airlift. The divers usually worked in an inverted position, but in some cases lots were not accessible from above because of the manner in which the wreckage had fallen and it was necessary to excavate in a more horizontal position, approaching the lot from an exposed side.

A significant but often overlooked advantage of the airlifts was that they could be utilized as a means of quick, convenient access to the areas being worked. In effect they were not unlike tethered life lines. They saved considerable time as it was not unusual for a diver without an airlift to orient him to spend 15 to 20 minutes locating his assigned lot by touch. The airlift provided a guide through the darkness as well as a convenient ladder for the divers' many trips to the surface during a shift for discussion and artifact transport (Fig. 10). They also prevented a descending or ascending diver from being carried away by the current during peak tide movement. As well, prior to the use of underwater communication systems in 1972, the airlifts were used to signal divers: surface crew would shut off the air supply and use a simple knocking code on the pipe to communicate with the divers.

The airlifts were generally removed from the water at the end of each working day. A diver would unfasten the weights on the base of the airlift and attach the lift to a large, balanced sling, and the lifts were all removed at once by crane. (Prior to 1971 the airlifts were pulled out by hand from the deck.) Replacing the airlift in the morning proved difficult, especially in strong currents, but a satisfactory technique was developed after much trial and error. At the surface a diver would tie a line to the intake end of his airlift and descend with the line to locate his assigned work area. On finding it, he would pull the line taut and the

10 Airlifts were utilized as a means of transit to and from the excavation points.

11 Airlifts discharging onto the sorting screens on an auxiliary barge. The boat-mounted hopper is alongside the barge.

12   Auxiliary airlift and compressor barges moored alongside the main support vessel.

deck crew would extend the airlift out and over the dive area. The diver would then give a sharp tug as a signal and the deck crew would release the airlift while maintaining a line on the discharge end so they could secure it on the barge after the intake was in place. The diver would then pull the intake down until it reached the bottom, invariably within five feet of his lot. This technique reduced airlift breakage and saved installation time.

On most underwater excavation sites, airlifts are allowed to discharge into the surrounding water. Because of the low to zero visibility at Restigouche, a surface airlift discharge system was developed that permitted a visual review of excavated material. This involved setting up an auxiliary barge where the discharge could be handled (Fig. 11).

Spoil was channelled by the discharged water from the deck of the barge into boat-mounted hoppers. After the spoil was checked, the boats dumped the spoil from the hoppers into the main river channel away from the site. The overall excavation set-up is depicted in Figures 12 and 13, showing the airlift installation and screening process.

Trash Pumps

Trash pumps, also called muck pumps, were employed to clear overburden in non-artifact-bearing areas. Two trash pumps, each with a capacity of 22 000 gallons per hour and capable of pumping 50-per-cent solids, were installed in the barge during the 1971 excavation season. The 60-foot intake hoses, which were four inches in diameter and made of heavy canvas-plyed rubber, were extremely heavy, cumbersome and generally difficult for divers to manipulate. Mounted on the intake ends

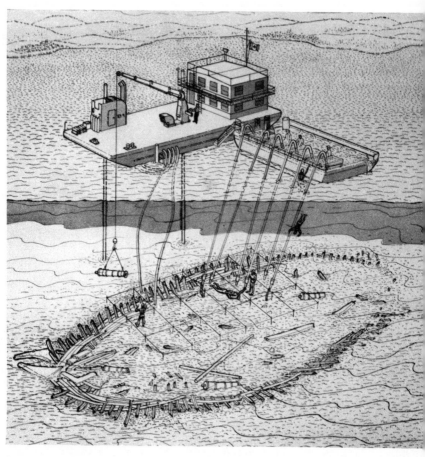

13 The final excavation set-up employed for the *Machault*.

of the hoses were safety grills and shut-off valves to prevent the diver's hands from being sucked into the hoses.

The total performance of the trash pumps as an excavation aid can best be described as poor. They continually jammed with bark and twigs and the installation of special "chopper" impellers for the 1972 season did nothing to improve their performance, nor did several intake modifications improve them. When the pumps were unobstructed, suction strength was satisfactory, but the divers could not maintain this unobstructed state. The only area where the trash pumps were even semi-useful was in clearing the soft, predominately mud mounds deposited by the downthruster, but the consensus of the divers was that the units were not efficient even there. The use of trash pumps as excavation tools is a sound concept and has been proven on other underwater sites, usually those with predominately sandy conditions;

however, their use at Restigouche, given the heterogeneous nature of its overburden, was far from successful.

Downthruster

The "downthruster" or "blower" (basically a propeller-driven vertical water thruster) was used primarily to investigate the boundaries of the site as well as to clear previously excavated areas that had silted in. This tool went through several evolutionary stages at Restigouche. The final version was a converted landing barge which had a 235-horsepower inboard engine with a modified foot (Fig. 14). The foot modification placed the propeller in a horizontal orientation that propelled a column of water downward. In operation, a 20-foot, 3/4-inch-diameter pipe attached to the barge close to the downthrusting unit was manoeuvred into position over the work area. The diver would then surface and signal to have the marker pipe raised and the downthrusting started. The diver remained on the surface while the downthruster operated, from a few minutes up to half an hour, depending on the type and amount of overburden, the depth of the water and the current. After it was shut down, the diver waited a few minutes for the disturbed sediment to clear, if any visibility was present, before descending to examine the extent of the clearing. A check was made for structural remains and artifacts, the downthruster was repositioned, and the operation was continued until the job was completed.

14   The modified foot of the downthruster.

A downthruster would normally be considered a salvage or testing tool that would have to be used judiciously in surveying areas of determining site boundaries. At Restigouche the downthruster was used extensively to clear previously excavated areas of hull so that sections could be cut and raised. In this capacity the downthruster saved hundreds of diving hours that would otherwise have been consumed in clearing the hull.

Hand and Pneumatic Tools

Concretions (rock-hard conglomerations of metal, mud, wood and/or any other immediate material) were commonly encountered attached or close to ferrous metal artifacts. Some individual concretions encompassed more than 300 cubic feet and were extremely costly in terms of excavation man-hours, but it was within the concretions that some of the best-preserved artifacts were found.

To break the concretions into manageable pieces that could be taken to the surface, the divers used various hand tools such as hammers, chisels, crowbars and pile-drivers. Developed on site, the pile-driver was a solid metal rod within a pipe sleeve. A "concretion chipper" was also developed on the project. Essentially, it was a two-foot-long metal pipe approximately one inch in diameter. A chisel was welded to one end and inserted into the other end was a smaller-diameter solid steel rod that slid up and down inside the pipe and provided the driving force. The length of the chipper also made it an effective crowbar. Although the chippers were easier to control and coordinate than other tools, they did not have the force of a hammer and chisel, and working with them was still tedious and exhausting. Hand tools of any type were effective on the looser material, but had practically no effect on the larger, firmly entrenched mounds of mortar bombs, cannonballs, bar shot, wrought-iron strappings, etc. Moreover, the chipping and prying methods endangered the artifacts within the concretions.

In an effort to accelerate the removal of the concretions, various pneumatic tools, such as jackhammers and drills, were experimented with. Powered by low-pressure compressors, they were effective in penetrating the concretions, but the risk of damage to artifacts was still present.

Underwater Explosives

In the later stages of the 1969 season, experiments were conducted in a method of breaking up concretions that would normally be considered anathema to archaeologists. The use of explosives to loosen concretions was introduced and proved so successful that it was continued in subsequent seasons. (Since then considerable research has been reported on the controlled use of explosives on underwater archaeological sites with commendable results [Green 1975].)

Charge sizes varied according to the extent and configuration of the concretion involved, but were normally limited to less than one-third of a standard stick of 40-per-cent Forcite, a low-velocity, gelatin-type high explosive. Detonation was accomplished by electric blasting caps wired to a blasting machine. Approximately 100 feet of lead-up wire was used. A manufacturer's representative recommended a non-electric detonating device for the 1972 season and he also suggested the use of Prima Cord, a high-velocity explosive in coil form, as a possible aid in severing timbers. Some preliminary experimentation, on discarded timber, with Prima Cord as a cutting agent was not successful and neither recommendation was ultimately instituted owing to the minimal requirements for explosives in 1972.

Basic detonation and safety procedures were followed. All divers were called to the surface and most of the barge electrical and mechanical equipment was shut down to prevent any possibility of accidental detonation. After a diver placed the primed charge, the powderman checked to ensure that all divers were out of the water before detonation. After waiting a few minutes for the sediment to clear, the diver returned to the blast site to verify the effect of the charge and to determine whether further charges were required.

Several different planting methods were tried, but results were difficult to analyze due to the lack of visibility, unknown subsurface conditions, etc. One of the more evidently effective techniques consisted of simply suspending the charge from the grid just above the target for shock waves alone were often effective in reducing concretions. In some instances, such as with a mound of concreted mortar shells, it was much more efficient to place a charge in direct contact with the concretions. The nature of the surrounding stratigraphy, ship's structure and type of artifacts involved (determined by sight and touch) were the critical factors in determining the placement of the charges.

Results were highly satisfactory. Whole artifacts, such as porcelain dishes and leather shoes, could be freed without damage and lumps of concretions still containing artifacts were reduced to easily handled sizes. The concretions generally broke along their natural formation lines around the artifacts, often revealing perfect moulds of the artifacts within them.

Given the conditions present, explosives were much less hazardous to artifacts than were concretion chippers, crowbars, or any other device used to excavate the concreted masses. The restraining effect of the water prevented any appreciable loss in provenience reference of the concretions. The saving in diving time was very great since other methods were fruitless with the more difficult concretions. The judicious use of explosives proved to be one of the most efficient, effective and least destructive excavation tools employed at Restigouche.

Underwater Communication System

In 1972 five Subcom single-side-band acoustic communication units were acquired for use underwater (Fig. 3) which, when coupled with a surface unit, provided full diver-to-surface, surface-to-diver and diver-to-diver communications. The wireless units allowed the divers to

maintain their freedom of movement without danger of becomin
entangled in wires in the low- or zero-visibility conditions. With th
surface unit, the safety diver on deck was able to maintain contact wit
any one of the divers. A diver could communicate directly with th
surface and with other divers, which was especially important o
multiple-man jobs. The acquisition of the system was a profoun
advancement in diving safety and speed of the work.

Submersible Chain Saws

During 1972 when work centred on raising sections of the *Mo
chault,* submersible hydraulic chain saws were employed to cut th
predominately oak timbers (see Fig. 15). Reciprocating twin-blad
pneumatic saws had been employed to cut intrusive logs on the site i
previous years, but they were not successful in their application t
continual underwater cutting of hardwood.

The two hydraulic saws' rated capacities were 500 gallons pe
minute at 1000 to 2000 psi at a chain speed of 3000 to 3500 fpm. A
extension handle was added to each saw to increase leverage and blade
of various lengths -- 12 inches, 18 inches and 24 inches -- were provide
to operate in restricted spaces, to get at hard-to-reach places and t
accommodate different thicknesses of wood. The power unit, designe
and built on the project, consisted of a deck-mounted hydraulic flui

15   Cross-hull cut being made on ceiling planking.

50

reservoir and pump powered by a 12-horsepower single-cylinder, four-cycle gasoline engine. Connecting the power unit with the saw were two 60-foot lengths of one-inch-diameter hydraulic hose.

Over 50 per cent of the sawing took place in absolute zero visibility, complicating procedures considerably and necessitating rigid safety precautions. Bulky protective overalls made from 1/4-inch ballistic nylon were worn over the operator's diving suit and, although they were cumbersome to move in, the protection they afforded warranted the inconvenience. All divers except the saw operator stayed away from the immediate sawing area. Specially constructed trigger guards on the saws ensured that they could only be operated when the diver was ready. The power unit was started when the operator signalled the deck crew that he was in position and it was always stopped when the diver was taking the saw down to the site, changing sawing locations or bringing the saw up for repair or change of chains or blades.

Generally speaking, the chain saws were extremely effective in cutting the timbers. The major problem was the constant dulling of the blades. Experiments with timber cut while not in contact with the river bottom showed that the saws could cut through a nine-inch-square hardwood frame in a matter of seconds without appreciable dulling, but most of the timber that was cut rested on the abrasive, dulling material of the surrounding riverbed. In addition, the space between the outer hull and the ceiling planking was often filled with sand, gravel and other dulling material. A diver could frequently cut only a matter of inches before he had to surface to change chains. A sharpened chain was mounted on the second saw so that it was only necessary to switch hydraulic connections in order to provide the diver with a sharp saw without an appreciable loss of time.

16 Ceiling planking cut between frames to permit access to the exterior planking.

Raising the Timbers of the *Machault*

In 1972 the following sections of the *Machault*'s hull were designated to be recovered for analysis and display: a cross-section of the hull, one frame thick, suitable for mounting on the wall of an interpretation centre; a length of keel/keelson assembly with about ten feet of framing and ceiling planking attached as a basis for a display of cargo stowage; a number of knees; any pieces, such as the rudder and stern assembly, which were considered of interest; and a quantity of miscellaneous timber and planking. In all, some 40 tons of structural material were designated for recovery and were ultimately raised.

The stern section of the hull was also to be investigated and selected structural elements recovered from that area. In previous years

17 Raising the lower port hull portion of the midsection. Even though the iron pins, fittings and spikes had rusted away, the wooden trunnels still held and the structure was strong enough to be self-supporting.

18 Raising the lower starboard stern hull section.

the port side of the wreck had been excavated for a distance of some 50 feet beyond the stern limit of the keelson. At that point there was no evidence of a discontinuation in the scattered ship's timbers; however, no major stern deadwood pieces had been identified and it seemed reasonable to assume that the starboard section of the stern might be rich in architectural details concerning this complex section of the ship (Waddell 1972: 8).

General Procedures

The majority of the cutting done consisted of cross-hull cuts made at right angles to the keelson (Fig. 15). Because of the double-skin construction, it was necessary to cut the ceiling planking the full width of the space between the frames (usually about nine inches) to get the chain saw between the frames to make the single cut required for the exterior hull planking (Fig. 15). Further, concretions, artifacts, sediment and debris had to be removed from between the inner and outer planking in order to reach the outer hull and this could only be done by removing the short length of inner planking between the frames (Fig. 16).

19 Monitoring the initial lift of the starboard railing section; the downthruster is in the background.

20 The secondary support barge being manoeuvred under the port stern section.

Following the cutting of the hull, the sections were lashed in such a manner as to permit them to be raised intact. The lashing method was usually dependent on the piece being lifted, but the major hull sections followed a general pattern. At the more prominent futtock end a 2-1/2-inch galvanized pipe was laid parallel to the planking and perpendicular to the frames. A rope was attached to the pipe and half-hitched in a stitching fashion along the pipe and encompassing the end of each frame successively. A sling or series of slings were then attached to evenly balanced points along the pipe so they pulled on the stitching ropes which pulled on the pipes in a binding or self-choking manner to clamp the frame ends more firmly (Figs. 17, 18) and avoid movement on the slippery wood. Although relatively simple in theory, it was not simple in practice. The frame ends were often buried and had to be cleared with the trash pump or airlifts prior to attaching the pipe. Often the frame ends could not be cleared enough and one or two inner and outer hull planks had to be removed to afford a securing point.

The average width of the sections raised (measuring at right angles to the planking) was approximately 11 feet. This narrow width enabled the divers to lace additional rope across the hull and around the frames at the other extremity of the section as extra security in the event that the primary lashings slipped.

Individual timbers were slung according to their particular configuration with 1-1/2-inch polypropylene rope. Depending on the object's weight, the rope was often doubled or tripled. Some of the heavier pieces were deeply imbedded in the river bottom sediment and in order to sling them properly, it was necessary to take a temporary purchase on the end or edge of the piece in order to tilt it to attach a sling at the timber's centre of buoyancy.

The hook of the main deck crane was attached to the slings' lift points and the slack taken up. The diver would then leave the immediate lift area and instruct the crane operator to begin applying tension to the cable. With most sections the lifting followed without any great complications. After the section was raised a few feet, the diver would halt the crane and check the progress, noting any attachment problems or sticking points. In some instances the partially lifted section would reveal a part of the hull that had not been sawn through or had not been readily visible until that stage and that required further cutting or manoeuvring prior to continuing the raising process.

The sections were raised in stages until they were clear of the river bottom. The initial lifting required more force to overcome the suction of the buried sections; however, once free of the bottom, the timbers had a relatively slight negative buoyancy which created some problems since such pieces exposed a large surface area to the strong currents. The submerged section was manoeuvred as close to the barge as possible to increase the mechanical advantage of the crane, then raised clear of the water. The loss of buoyancy as well as the shifting due to currents made this one of the most complex parts of the entire operation. Normally a rope was tied to the section so that the deck crew could control any undue swinging when the current became a secondary factor to the prevailing wind.

As rising timbers broke the surface, the hitches had to be constantly monitored (Fig. 19) because of the additional strain due to decreased buoyancy, surface wave action and the wind factor affecting the suspended timber. If serious shifting did occur, it was sometimes necessary to attach additional strapping or to lower the timber and relash it completely. This was especially true of the pieces which had initially been tied in zero visibility where the weight and extent of the piece had to be estimated by feeling the unburied portion. If the raised section was not a major piece, that is, less than two tons, the crane could manoeuvre it onto the deck of one of the main support barges. If the section was a major one, the crane could not handle the weight at any great extension and so instead of moving the section to the support, the support was brought to the section by manoeuvring a barge under it (Fig. 20) with the crane operating at greatest mechanical advantage.

Bow Section

The first major task undertaken in 1972 was the recovery of the bulk of the bow structure as well as the rudder, upper sternpost and other timbers stored within the ship's hull. All of these pieces had originally been raised for examination and recording in 1971, then returned to the hull until conservation procedures were finalized and facilities prepared in 1972.

It was first necessary to clear the accumulated silt and overburden which had filled in the previously excavated hull. With the use of the downthruster, this task was greatly accelerated. This was attributed to the curvature of the central hull which formed a concavity that deflected the propeller wash out of the hull, carrying the silt with it. Following the clearing, the stored bow timbers were recovered; their original recovery in 1971 is reported below.

The major fore and aft timbers (the sternpost-keel intersection and the keel-stem-head assembly) were over 100 feet apart and had fallen to the port side of the wreck. In falling to port, these structural sections had twisted and broken the keel at both ends, the break being complete in the bow but only partial in the stern.

The bow sections raised consisted of two major parts: the stem-head assembly, which also included the apron and knee of the head as well as gammoning and bobstay pieces, and the stem-gripe assembly, which included the forwardmost section of keel. No cutting was required prior to raising either piece as they had both been severed in the natural breakup of the ship. Both the upper and lower stems remained virtually intact as they had broken away from the attaching timbers at an original joint.

The stem-head section was almost completely silted over when originally located. The area surrounding this section was excavated prior to tilting the section off bottom at the upper hull end to lash it for raising. Visibility was zero during this operation, but fortunately the divers could feel the gammoning holes and were able to place rope through them, as well as around other associated timbers, preventing the

21 The stem-head section being raised.

22 Rope sling around the stem-keel scarph of the stem-gripe assembly. Stopwaters in the scarph are still in place.

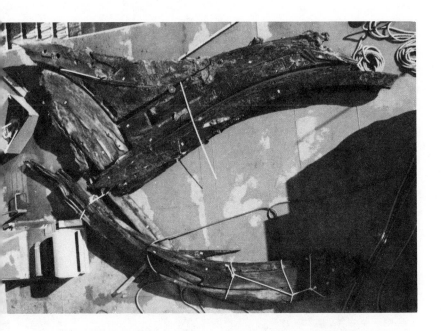

23 The stem-head and stem-gripe assemblies on the support barge.

loss of some of the remaining components of the upper bow structural unit The section was lifted (Fig. 21) with all the components that had been attached *in situ*. Two pieces of the extreme upper structure, the timber containing the bobstay holes and the timber immediately above the one bearing the gammoning holes, were also recovered. Both pieces, as well as the extreme upper limit of the sternpost, showed significant marine growth, indicating that for the most part they had protruded above silt level. Their exposure to currents and the degenerative effects of the water accounted for the accelerated breakdown of their pinnings. This is especially well illustrated in comparing the upper extremity of the stem-head section, which has lost all its sharp lines and shows extreme signs of erosion, with the sections immediately below, which, being below silt level, retain clean, sharp edges with the ferrous pinning still relatively intact (Fig. 21).

The lower bow section or stem-gripe assembly presented no particular difficulties. Its lower end was below the bow or south end of the keelson (see Fig. 9). Temporary ropes lifted the section clear enough of the bottom to permit the attachment of a rope sling at critical stress points, such as the lower stem-keel scarph (Fig. 22). The stem-gripe assembly was then moved northward, out from below the keelson, and up to the surface (Fig. 23). The entire lower cutwater section had been preserved several feet below silt level, consequently the structural integrity of the scarph joints was reasonably well maintained (Fig. 22) and this section was raised intact.

24 The heel of the *Machault*. The heel strap abutting the lowest gudgeon reinforced the mortise and tenon of the keel and sternpost.

Stern Section

Raising sections of the stern hull and deadwood was greatly simplified by as-found breaks and separations in these areas. Two other factors simplifying the cutting were a relative dearth of inner hull planking and the fact that much of the area cut was beyond the stern limit of the keelson and therefore no compound keel-keelson cutting, such as that done in the midsection, was required. Five sections of hull

25 Cross-section of the stern keel cut. The keel is 14 inches in height.
The orientation of the garboard rabbet is almost vertical.

were recovered from this area, three from the port side and two from
the starboard.

The heel of the ship (Fig. 24), formed by the mortising of the
sternpost into the keel and reinforced with a knee, had fallen approximately 60 degrees to port. The keel had borne the brunt of the fall; it
had twisted and broken almost through at a point approximately 22 feet
from the keel-sternpost intersection. This twisted area was under much
fallen timber and it was decided to sever the keel aft of this point,
giving a total cut-keel length of 20 feet. (See Figure 25 for a cross-
section view of the stern keel cut.) The keel-sternpost section presented
no great difficulties in either lashing it or raising it, and it was lifted
intact (Fig. 24).

26 The upper end of the broken sternpost. The incised draught marks are similar to those on the stem.

27   Raising the 31-foot-long rudder.

The other sections of the stern were recovered with relative ease. It was felt that enough was raised from the port stern to permit a frame reconstruction from the keel to the topmost futtock.

Two major structural pieces had been recovered from the stern in 1971: the uppermost end of the broken sternpost showing the ship's draught in Roman numerals (Fig. 26) and the 31-foot-long rudder (Fig. 27). Figure 9 illustrates the locations from which the upper sternpost and rudder were originally recovered in 1971; both had been stored within the ship's hull through the winter of 1971-72.

Midsection

A midsection swath with a minimum width of twelve feet was recovered from the central hull. Cuts, at right angles to the keel, were made between the futtocks and through the extant hull structure. The cuts encompassed the area of the keelson in which the mainmast had been stepped and beside which the pumps had been fitted.

Four major sections were recovered from the midsection. The port-most section and the two starboard sections presented no particular

28   The cradle being secured to the inverted keelson hull section. (Th
keel has been removed.)

problems in cutting or raising; however, the keelson section, measurir
approximately 20 feet port to starboard, presented difficulties.

Better than two weeks of preparation were necessary before a
attempt at lifting the keelson section could be made.   After dowr
thrusting the area, a quantity of heavy munitions, primarily cannonbal
and mortar bombs, had to be removed from the ceiling planking of th
keelson section.   Cutting was complicated by the keel-keelson assembl
it was necessary to cut a 12-inch block out of the keelson to reach th
keel, and having cut the keelson, the diver had to lie face down on th
ceiling planking, extending his arms down through the floors to bring th
chain saw into contact with the keel.

When the keel cuts were believed to be complete (they could not b
reached by hand), an attempt was made to lift the section.   This prove
to be extremely difficult due to the magnitude of the section and th
narrowness of the cuts, approximately 3/8 of an inch wide, through th
outer planking.   The section tended to bind on the fore and aft parts e
the hull from which it was being extracted.   Attempts to raise it had
be interrupted because additional cutting was required or because th
lift angle had to be changed to prevent the timbers from binding, but
was finally lifted intact except for a small keel fragment which wa
later recovered.

It quickly became evident that it was beyond the capacity of th
deck crane (13-ton maximum) to raise the keelson section out of th
water: it was the heaviest piece cut, as well as one of the mo

29   The keelson section of the hull with the cradle secured to its underside, ready for raising.

structurally complex. It would have to be towed underwater to larger crane facilities and a rigid cradle would have to support it when it was lifted clear of the water. The rigid cradle was the only reasonable solution to maintaining the structural integrity of the keelson section.

Four 12-inch-by-16-inch timbers were lap-joined and pinned at the corners to form a rectangular box 11 feet by 13 feet which would accommodate the keelson section. Installation of the cradle was complicated by the fact that the cradle would require a great deal of ballast to sink and, secondly, that it was not possible to manoeuvre the section into a position that would allow the cradle to be attached to it. It was decided to turn the keelson over and raise it in an inverted position so the cradle could be attached to its underside at the surface. Trebled ropes were attached around the now-inverted section and it was returned to the bottom. The cradle was then floated into position above the section, the crane hook was lowered through the cradle, and the section was pulled to the surface (Fig. 28). After the cradle was secured, the section was again lowered to the bottom, the crane hook was attached to one end of the unit and the entire unit was then partially raised and reinverted to its original position with the cradle now underneath. The cradle and keelson section were then lashed and raised to the surface (Fig. 29) where a final check was made before the entire unit was slung below an auxiliary barge for towing to a local deepwater wharf. There a 25-ton mobile crane raised the unit and placed it on a float for transfer to the preservation shed.

Part Three
Summary of Findings

Walter Zacharchuk

The *Machault* was sunk in the navigable channel, with its port bow portion farthest downstream and lower in the mud than its starboard side. The starboard bow of the ship appeared to have been sheared off, probably by ice action. Since the ebb tide is stronger than the flow, artifacts that were moved about by tides and ice concentrated in the pocket formed by the collapsed port bow and were then silted over. Excavation began in this portion of the ship and only limited areas under and outside the hull were investigated. In the last year of excavation, during a rare break in the almost constantly poor visibility that hampered work on the site, divers saw a large deposit of material, once contained in the hold, outside the excavation area on the port (downstream) side of the wreck. The excavation was not expanded to include this area because of time constraints.

Excavation of the *Machault* had been envisioned as a controlled salvage operation with three goals: to enrich our understanding of the Battle of the Restigouche, to provide data on maritime architecture of the mid-18th century, and to retrieve artifacts in use at a known date. Work on the *Machault* has met these goals.

We now have a clearer understanding of the battle events: that the *Machault* was positioned across the navigable channel in an effort to protect the other elements of the French fleet and that, when the situation appeared hopeless, it had been evacuated of personnel and their possessions, and other objects had been removed.

From study of retrieved pieces of the hull of the ship, it is possible to verify that fire damaged the *Machault* from midsection on the port side forward toward the bow. The top of the bilge pump, tops of the ribs and top of the forepeak are charred; the figurehead, if there was one, is missing and was presumably consumed by the fire. The standing rigging is charred and had fallen into the hull of the ship. All this supports historical accounts of a fire on board the *Machault* and of seven feet of water in its hold. Given the height of the July tides, the *Machault* would have been sitting on the river bottom when the tide was out.

History also records an explosion on board. At one point during work on the site, a portion of decking was observed approximately 400 feet from the starboard side of the ship. The decking showed some evidence of explosion — wrenched timbers and charring — however, it cannot be definitely ascribed to the *Machault* and no other archaeological evidence could be found to substantiate an explosion on board.

The ship's reconstruction on paper will define the basic and superficial aspects of the structure, but the study of assembly and structural details will not be completed until parts of the ship are physically reconstructed at a future date. (Complete reconstruction of the entire vessel was never a goal of the project.) Historical records of its performance suggest that the ship was a fast sailer, but architectural aspects that would either confirm or deny this have not been recovered.

It has not been possible from the excavated material and the as-found remains of the ship to develop a complete picture of the *Machault* as it appeared when the French abandoned and sank it; nevertheless, an enormous amount of material culture remains was recovered during the excavation.

The unexpected wealth of material made it necessary to develop sophisticated procedures and facilities, as well as to train personnel, to deal with the site, expertise that has been applied to other more or less complicated sites. The quantity of repetitive material has also allowed some experimentation of a potentially destructive nature in order to develop and test new conservation treatments. The underwater environment has preserved organic materials to a degree not encountered on land sites under normal circumstances. (The excellent state of preservation of the cargo applied equally to the ship's timbers and structural parts.) Since the ship was inaccessible for salvage at the time of its sinking, objects that seldom appear in an assemblage from a land site such as copper or brass pots that could be reworked when they broke and lighting devices that usually had a long life span, have been retrieved and now form a part of Parks Canada's National Reference Collection.

In an attempt to anticipate what cargo was carried by the Machault, a search was made in French archives for a lading list of stores and cargo for its final voyage, but no complete inventory was found. Since each vessel of the original six ships of the fleet was a self sufficient operating unit, the Machault would have had on board munitions, food, food-related preparation, serving and consuming items, tools for operating the ship, spare parts, and other stores necessary to complete a 60- to 90-day voyage, as well as the personal effects of each person aboard and the ship's share of the fleet's cargo. The extent to which the crown supplied each individual's necessities, such as food, clothing, tobacco, tools and furniture, and how much of these were supplemented privately is not known. Nor can we be certain of the exact number of people who were aboard, although Ross (1981: Table 1) has estimated the Machault's population to have been 278 to 337, of which approximately 150 would have been sailors. Crew members on the Machault are unlikely to have had many possessions with them although some might have had some personal property, such as clothing, amusements, and any goods that they intended to trade in North America for profit. For men with very little private space on board ans with limited finances, trade goods would have been small and inexpensive: highly polished pieces of brass or copper, small silver objects, buckles, sewing goods, jewellery and ornaments. The ship's officers would have had their own larger spaces for storing their goods. The value and number of their possessions would have depended on their means and rank, but could have included furniture, table settings, and anything else necessary for their comfort and status.

Parks Canada's intent in excavating the Machault was to retrieve a representation of the cargo and structure of the wreck, not to excavate the site in its entirety. However, it became clear that some types of artifacts that could have been expected to be found on a ship were not present. Archaeologists and material culture researchers have noted a deficiency in the assemblages of cooking equipment, mess kits, lanterns, cannons and small arms, tools, navigational equipment, medical and religious paraphernalia (such as the religious symbols that often adorned the walls in sleeping areas on ships), provisions, chests and other furniture, and artifacts related to personal hygiene. Many of the missing goods are those that relate to everyday human activity. The absence of some of these objects can perhaps be explained by the fire and explosion on the ship and by the need to provision and protect the land camp.

It also became clear that some unexpected types and quantities of artifacts were present. Some cargo items — English and Chinese porcelains and French wineglasses — were concluded to have been privately owned and intended for private trade.

The artifacts recovered in the excavation appear to be ship-related structural elements and operating features, and cargo and other objects that would not be useful in a land-based camp. Personal goods appear in small numbers that suggest they had been lost or broken and discarded; several of these have obvious indications of use and some would, in 1760, have been considered old-fashioned. Nevertheless, although it is obvious that the ship was not in possession of its full complement of equipment and cargo when it went down, the ship has yielded a large and diversified selection of mid-18th-century goods, and the *Machault* collection, along with other tightly dated material from other sites, can be used as a period standard for dating and ascribing material from French-occupied sites with comparable occupation periods.

Bibliography

Beattie, Judith
1968.   The Battle of the Restigouche. Manuscript Report Series No.
19, pp. 1-135. Parks Canada, Ottawa.

Beattie, Judith, and Bernard Pothier
1977.   "The Battle of the Restigouche." Canadian Historic Sites:
Occasional Papers in Archaeology and History, No. 16, pp. 5-34. Ottawa.

Green, Jeremy N.
1975.   "The VOC Ship Batavia Wrecked in 1629 on the Houtman
Abrolhos, Western Australia." The International Journal of Nautical
Archaeology and Underwater Exploration, Vol. 4, Part 1 (March), pp. 43-
63. London.

Lanctôt, Gustave
1965.   A History of Canada. Trans. Margaret M. Cameron. Clarke,
Irwin, Toronto. Vol. 3: From the Treaty of Utrecht to the Treaty of
Paris, 1713-1763.

Litalien, Raymonde
1972.   "Le Machault, bateau corsaire du XVIIIe." Culture Vivante, No.
24 (March), pp. 11-16. Quebec.
1977.   "Le Machault de Bayonne, Frégate Corsaire échouée au Canada
en 1760." Bulletin de la Société des Sciences, Lettres et Arts de
Bayonne, No. 133, pp. 199-218. Bayonne.

Lower, Arthur R.M.
1949.   Colony to Nation; A History of Canada. 2nd ed. Longmans,
Green and Company, Toronto.

Maupassant, Jean de
1915.   Les armateurs bordelais au XVIIIe siècle; les deux expéditions
de Pierre Desclaux au Canada (1759 et 1760). Imprimeries Gounouilhou,
Bordeaux.

McNally, Paul
1977.   "Table Glass from the Wreck of the Machault." Canadian
Historic Sites: Occasional Papers in Archaeology and History, No. 16,
pp. 35-44. Ottawa.

Morton, William Lewis
1963.   The Kingdom of Canada; A General History from Earliest
Times. McClelland and Stewart, Toronto.

Proulx, Gilles
1979.   "The Machault: Some Research Notes and New Source Documents." Research Bulletin No. 110. Parks Canada, Ottawa.

Ross, Lester A.
1981.   "Eighteenth-Century French Naval Duties as Reflected by the Tools Recovered from Le Machault, a 5th-Rate Frigate Sunk in Chaleur Bay, Quebec, AD 1760." Manuscript on file, National Historic Parks and Sites Branch, Parks Canada, Ottawa.

Trudel, Marcel
1968.   Initiation à la Nouvelle-France. Holt, Rinehart, Winston. Montreal.

Waddell, Peter J.A.
1972.   "Proposal for the Selective Raising and Excavation of French Supply Ships in Restigouche." Manuscript on file, National Historic Parks and Sites Branch, Parks Canada, Ottawa.

Whate, R.E.
1979a.   "Chinese Export Porcelain from the Wreck of the Machault, 1760." Manuscript on file, National Historic Parks and Sites Branch, Parks Canada, Ottawa.
1979b.   "English Soft Paste Porcelain from the Wreck of the Machault, 1760." Manuscript on file, National Historic Parks and Sites Branch, Parks Canada, Ottawa.

Wilson, A.E.
1970.   "A Winter Survey with Proton Magnetometers of an Underwater Site." Prospezioni archeologiche, Vol. 5, pp. 89-94. Rome.